ESSENTIAL
ADVENT

Holy Moments and Sacred Experiences
for Your Whole Congregation

Aimée J. Jannsohn, Editor

Copyright © 2014 by Open Waters Publishing
All rights reserved.

Open Waters Publishing
700 Prospect Avenue
Cleveland, Ohio 44115
www.openwaterspublishing.com

Aimée J. Jannsohn, editor
Design by Robyn Henderson Nordstrom

Printed in the United States of America

First Edition: October 2014

10 9 8 7 6 5 4 3 2 1

Open Waters Publishing is an imprint of The Pilgrim Press.
The Open Waters Publishing name and logo are trademarks
of Local Church Ministries, the United Church of Christ.

ISBN 978-0-8298-2010-2

CONTENTS

Activities for Older Children (Ages 7–11)

Activities for Younger Children (Ages 3-6)

Activities for Intergenerational Groups

Activities for Seekers and Those New to Church

Worship Resources for Advent and Christmas

FOREWORD

Advent is a journey. From the sparkling flame of the first candle lit, to the Silent Night commemorated on Christmas Eve. It's a journey for which we know the destination as well as how we're going to get there. (It's only four weeks, after all.)

Essential Advent: Holy Moments and Sacred Experiences for Your Whole Congregation will help make your Advent journey more meaningful. It contains activities specially designed to fit every age group and individual faith journey you'll find in your congregation: children of all ages, youth, young adults, adults, intergenerational groups, and even those seeking a church home. It's hard to find something as all-encompassing in one volume.

Advent is all about tradition, and in *Essential Advent* you'll find worship resources for Advent givens like hanging of the greens and weekly lighting of Advent candles. You'll also be introduced to some traditions from around the world, such as the Mexican *Las Posadas*. And how cool would it be to learn about and celebrate "Christmas in India"—recipes included?

Travel through this season as you do each year, waiting and hoping, anticipating the grand finale—the birth of Jesus on Christmas Day. But perhaps you'll discover on the pages of *Essential Advent* ways to fill the days and weeks leading up to that day with more wonder and splendor and joy than ever before.

Peace be with you as you await the baby Jesus, Savior of the World.

Aimée J. Jannsohn, editor

ACTIVITIES FOR
ADULTS

The activities in this chapter will be most meaningful
for adults who are active in the life of their
congregation and knowledgeable about the seasons of
the church year, especially Advent and Christmas.

INSIDE *LAS POSADAS*

Leader preparation: Review the activity and consider your reactions. Gather materials and print words on newsprint or an erasable board.

Supplies:

- Bibles
- script: *Las Posadas* Reenactment, page 13

Ask volunteers to read aloud John 13:1–7, 31b–35 and Acts 2:42–47. Have the group identify ways that hospitality is given or received in each passage. Form two groups. Assign one scripture passage to each group. Challenge each group to create a presentation that convinces the other group that their passage makes the best case to view hospitality as a legitimate, year-round practice for any disciple. If time permits, reverse the passages and have each group make a case for the other passage.

Distribute the *Las Posadas* script. Print the simplified dialogue on an erasable board, or project it. Follow the instructions for the *Las Posadas* observance. Discuss together what it felt like to be rejected, to be the ones who rejected and then accepted, and to be the ones accepting. Why is it significant to our story that Jesus was born under such circumstances of inhospitality and then hospitality?

Invite a volunteer to read aloud Genesis 18:1–15. Ask: What would have happened if Abram had shut the door on the visitors? How does this sense of welcoming a stranger inspire an understanding that God may be a stranger to us at times? What does it take for us to welcome God by our welcome of others? Discuss the threat to us, if any, when a stranger approaches. What is a realistic response? Why? How can we distinguish between a legitimate caution and one that creates a barrier to the genuine presence of God in another person? How can we deal with the notion of threat in a creative and productive fashion?

LAS POSADAS REENACTMENT

Distribute candles to those in the group who represent the crowd that travels with Mary and Joseph. The roles of Joseph and the innkeeper can be played by a number of people at the same time.

Mary is pregnant and weary, as is Joseph who stops at designated places and knocks at the door to ask:

Joseph: In the name of God, we ask those who dwell here to give some travelers lodging this evening.

Innkeeper: This is not an inn. Move on. I cannot open lest you be a scoundrel.

As Joseph progresses through the designated sites of shelter, *posada*, the crowd of innkeepers becomes angrier. The couple grows even wearier, and Joseph begins to beg.

Joseph: We are tired from traveling from Nazareth. I am a carpenter named Joseph.

Finally, hoping for compassion, Joseph reveals Mary's identity as the Queen of Heaven. But this does not inspire a welcome.

Joseph: The Queen of Heaven is with me.

Have the group move around the learning space eight times to represent eight days and nights, and repeat this scene. Finally, on the ninth evening (Christmas Eve), Joseph reached an innkeeper who gives the couple a stable. Because of the love and compassion of this innkeeper, this place becomes not only the birthplace of Jesus, but is gloriously lit to be a place of beauty. In celebration of the birth of Jesus, the crowd breaks into song and dance and festival. Treats of all kinds, including the fun of a piñata, are enjoyed by all. This reminds the children that the stranger at the door can be God in disguise.

LAS POSADAS

Leader preparation: *Las Posadas* is an annual Mexican Advent ritual of rejection and welcome through the story of Mary and Joseph looking for a place to stay in Bethlehem. Learn about it on the Internet or through your public library or an international institute near you. Then plan a family celebration of *Las Posadas*.

Supplies:

- costumes
- food
- a piñata

As you make plans for a *Las Posadas* celebration, include a piñata, a favorite part of the celebration for children. If you do this at home, go from room to room. Or, if your family lives close, go from one family residence to another. When have you experienced welcome and rejection?

Resources:

The Night of Las Posadas by Tomie de Paola

Las Posadas: An Hispanic Christmas Celebration by Diane Hoyt-Goldsmith

Uno, Dos, Tres, Posada! (Spanish edition) by Virginia Kroll

RECYCLED BLESSINGS FOR MEALTIMES: AN AT-HOME ACTIVITY

Supplies:

- greeting cards you've received
- basket

Throughout the course of a year, most people receive a variety of greeting cards. It's a common tradition to send cards to acknowledge various life transitions and celebrations including birthdays, illness, death of a loved one, anniversaries, births, new jobs, graduations, retirements, Christmas and other holidays, and so on. Gather greeting cards that you and members of your household have received. Place them in a basket and set them on the table where you gather for meals. When you eat a meal together, have a family member choose a card from the basket and pray a prayer of blessing upon the person(s) who sent the card. Consider making this a "new tradition" by recycling old greeting cards into prayers of blessing.

GIFT AND BLESSING EXCHANGE

Leader preparation: This activity utilizes a portion of the apostle Paul's letter to the church in Rome: Romans 15:22–29. In this passage, Paul touches on a principal that strongly relates to Christian mission. We might call it "mutual indebtedness" or "mutual blessing." Paul pointed out the eagerness of the Gentile Christians of Macedonia and Achaia to donate and send money to those who were poor among the Jewish Christians in Jerusalem (v. 26). In Paul's mind that was fitting in that the Gentile Christians were in a sense responding to what they had received from their brothers and sisters of Jewish lineage. It was through the spiritual generosity of the Jewish Christians that the Gentiles had received the message of Christ. Paul extends this idea of mutual indebtedness—or mutual blessing—even further by suggesting that he would like to come to Rome and be "sent on" by the believers there to further missionary work in Spain. (v. 24). There is little if any difference between Paul's expectation of Christian behavior and what Jesus expressed when he said, "From everyone to whom much has been given, much will be required; and from the one to whom much has been entrusted, even more will be demanded" (Luke 12:48). Among the things that propel us in Christian mission is the desire to pass on the blessing that has been bestowed upon us.

Supplies:

- Bibles
- markers and whiteboard or newsprint

Form two groups. Identify one group as the Gift Initiators. The role of the Gift Initiators will be to come up with a gift they would like to give to members of the other group. Identify the second group as the Gift Responders. The role of the Gift Responders will be to "receive" the gift of the Gift Initiators and then determine what they would like to give to the Gift Initiators in return. For example, gift exchanges might be something like the following:

- The Gift Initiators give the Gift Responders a new SUV. In return the Gift Responders give the Gift Initiators a new minivan.
- The Gift Initiators give the Gift Responders the wish for long life and happiness.

In return the Gift Responders give the Gift Initiators the wish for peace and prosperity.

- The Gift Initiators give the Gift Responders a toaster oven. In return the Gift Responders give the Gift Initiators an espresso machine.
- The Gift Initiators give the Gift Responders a new book. In return the Gift Responders give the Gift Initiators a CD of favorite songs.

Write two headings on the whiteboard or newsprint: "Initial Gift" and "Response Gift."

As the two groups offer their suggested gifts, write their gifts under the appropriate heading. After a few rounds from the Gift Initiators and the Gift Responders, reverse the roles and ask the Initiators to become the Responders and the Responders to become the Initiators for a few exchanges. As a group, look at what is written on the whiteboard or newsprint. Invite any comments that participants would like to make about the exercise. In particular, ask if any observation can be made about the gifts that were suggested in response to the initial gifts.

One pattern that could emerge from this exercise is that the Gift Responders will likely attempt to give gifts to the Gift Initiators that are similar in value or intrinsic "wow" factor to the gifts given to them. We see this kind of impulse in Christmas giving. Many people give considerable thought to giving a gift that is commensurate in value with the gift they think they will get from a particular person. If someone is likely to give them a bottle of imported champagne, for example, they aren't likely to plan to give in return a thirty-cents-off coupon from the House of Greasy Burgers.

Ask the following questions:

To what extent is it reasonable to feel a desire to give others a gift that is similar in value to a gift they have given to us?

To what extent should gift giving be free of a desire to respond in kind to the gifts given to us by others?

Ask a volunteer to read aloud Romans 15:22–29. Pose the following questions for discussion:

At what points in this passage do you perceive a sense of mutual blessing?

As followers of Christ, to what extent should we feel an impulse or responsibility to "pass the blessing on?" What role, if any, should this impulse play in how we respond to God's call to mission?

To what extent should actions taken to pass the blessing on be motivated from a sense of responsibility or a joyous desire to bless as we have been blessed?

ACTIVITIES FOR
YOUNG ADULTS

The following activities focus on Advent traditions
and rituals that will engage this busy,
multi-tasking group no matter how familiar they may
be with this holy season.

SPECIAL CARE FOR CHILDREN DURING THE CHRISTMAS SEASON

Leader preparation: Think about opportunities for providing special care for children within your church or community. How does your church provide care for its children? Do you have a Safe Sanctuary program in place? How are the children's areas furnished? What is your congregation's policy for children and communion? What accommodations are made for children at all-church events, such as worship and fellowship dinners? See the ideas below and add these to any opportunities your church already offers or any you know about. If the ideas are new to your congregation, think about beginning a tradition of reaching out to help children through activities like these. How would the tradition benefit the children? The young adults?

Supplies:

None

Invite the group to think about how they can use their time, talents, and money to help children, who are usually the most vulnerable persons in any society. Talk about the opportunities your church offers and describe how these opportunities fit as tradition. Discuss any opportunities your church may not have tried. Ask the young adults to think about how they might reach out to children. These deliberations require the participants to practice discernment regarding their priorities. Encourage the group to commit to do at least one of the activities discussed or following and decide dates for the activity. How will they keep one another informed of what everyone is doing? How will they hold themselves accountable?

HOLIDAY GIFTS FOR CHILDREN

Locate a school or preschool in which numerous families need assistance providing holiday gifts for children. Talk with that school's administrator or social worker to supply first names and three gift suggestions for children in need. Hang these names and gift suggestions on a Christmas tree. Ask church adults, including young adults, to select the name of one or more children, obtain one of the requested gifts, and bring the gift to church by a certain date. See that young adults deliver the gifts to the school prior to the beginning of the holiday recess so that they can be distributed by school personnel.

SPEND TIME WITH HOSPITALIZED CHILDREN

Find out from a local hospital if they allow volunteers to provide respite care for parents of children. Perhaps there's a neonatal unit where infants live for several weeks following birth. Or there may be a hospital or a hospital division in which children live who are undergoing long-term treatment. Young adults may volunteer to spend time with these children when their parents take rest periods. Visits could include rocking the babies, telling stories, singing, and playing games.

IT'S ALL IN THE VERSE

Leader preparation: How many Christmas hymns can you name off the top of your head? Make a list. How many of these hymns can you connect to Luke 1:39–56? How many can you connect to John 12:20–36 (more difficult)? Choose a few hymns from your list, locate them in a hymnal of your choice, and review their verses ahead of time.

Supplies:
- index cards
- pens
- (optional) hymnals

Provide hymnals so students can look up the Christmas hymns you chose and review the verses. Have them choose a line or phrase from one of the hymns and write it on an index card. Tell them to keep the card in their wallet or purse until next week, or tape it to a mirror where they can see it when they get ready each morning. Next week, have them discuss how many times they thought of that verse because of something that happened during their day.

RECLAIMING RELIGIOUS HOLY DAYS

Leader preparation: A great tradition of the church is the celebration of the birth of Jesus. This is also a secular holiday celebrated around the world. Think about the ways that the secular and religious expressions are different. Consider how they are the same.

Supplies:

- Bible

Read Isaiah 52:7–10 to the class. Ask students to reflect on and discuss the following questions:

What do you think it means to spread the good news?

What good news can we share at Christmas?

Reflect on possible things you can do or say that might give witness to your faith in Jesus Christ during the holiday season.

How might you celebrate Christmas differently as a testimony and witness to your faith?

How can you let others know what these days mean to you?

Encourage students to put their ideas into practice this year.

TWELVE DAYS OF SPIRITUAL GIFTS

Leader preparation: "The Twelve Days of Christmas" is a popular carol heard during the seasons of Advent and Christmas. It tells of a dozen gifts being given to one's true love, including a partridge in a pear tree. Since the song is either English or French in origin, the gifts date back to an earlier time in history. In this activity, the group is asked to update the song for this modern era by coming up with twelve spiritual gifts they could give to a significant other. To prepare, it can be helpful to review the background information on the "The Twelve Days of Christmas" carol found on Wikipedia.

Supplies:
- song: "The Twelve Days of Christmas"
- music player
- markers and newsprint or whiteboard

Play a recording of the "The Twelve Days of Christmas" for the group, and ask for some thoughts on what these gifts might have looked like, what they represented, or how they might have been received. Invite the group to come up with their own collection of twelve presents, with one difference: the gifts are to be spiritual gifts they'd like to give to a good friend or family member. Consider the following questions and record their "Twelve Spiritual Gifts" on the newsprint or whiteboard:

What would the gifts be?

What's the thinking behind their choices of gifts?

If you had all day to celebrate each gift, how would you do it?

If the size of the group allows, form two or three smaller groups of participants, and have them think of up to three activities for each day that would help them celebrate and cherish that particular gift for ministry. These gifts and activities could be anything they wish—encourage them to be extremely creative. After they come up with ideas, have them come back together as a group to share their thoughts.

NO NAÏVE NATIVITY

Leader preparation: Be ready for the participant who may remind the group that the scripture story of the nativity is different from the sets we put out at Christmas. This is accurate, but the nativity set helps us tell the story, and today it will help us reflect on the different characters in the story.

Supplies:
- nativity set (crèche)
- markers and newsprint or whiteboard
- paper and pen

Set up the nativity in the middle of the group and ask the participants to look at each human figure and think about how it would have felt physically to be "in their shoes" the night Jesus was born. List each character on newsprint or whiteboard, and next to each name, write the group's responses. For example, the shepherds could have been tired and anxious, or eager and excited. Mary probably had swollen feet and was experiencing contractions, then went through the pain of childbirth. Save Jesus for last.

Use the following questions to further the discussion:

Who do you think was the most uncomfortable person in the nativity scene?

As you look at the list of physical experiences, when in Jesus' life did he feel or experience things that others felt at the time of his birth?

When have you felt the things on the list?

How does it make you feel to know Jesus felt many of the same physical struggles and joys that we feel?

How does this change the way we pray or what we pray about?

As a group retell the Christmas story in a way that focuses on the physical experience of the night. Write it down, share it with other groups, and offer it as a reading for Advent worship.

CHRISTMAS PAGEANT

Leader preparation: One of the most sacred traditions in many churches is the annual children's Christmas pageant. Many lifelong members find a blessing of comfort and peace in its consistent message and youthful portrayal. This tradition often includes pieces of the Gospels of Matthew and Luke. In this activity, young adults are encouraged to "dissect" a traditional children's Christmas pageant to learn both what this tradition highlights of the birth of Jesus and what it fails to communicate.

Supplies:

- three or four copies of a traditional Christmas pageant that includes shepherds and wise men, such as the free one available online at Doubleestudios.com.
- Bibles
- highlighter pens

As young adults gather, form two groups: a "Matthew" group and a "Luke" group. Distribute Bibles and give each group one or two copies of the pageant script. Direct the "Matthew" group to read Matthew 1:18–2:12 and highlight portions of the script that pertain to these verses. Have them note what information or events from these verses are missing from the script. Direct the "Luke" group to read Luke 1:26–2:20 and highlight portions of the script that pertain to these verses. Have them note what information or events from these verses are missing from the script.

Give groups about fifteen minutes to work, and then ask them to report their findings to the entire group.

Questions for discussion:

Why do you think there's a difference between the Gospels and the script?

Why is some information left out of the pageant? What messages are congregations missing because those parts of the stories are missing?

Why are details added to the script that aren't in the Gospels? (e.g., the number of wise men) How important are these details to the meaning of the story?

What are the advantages and disadvantages to having a tradition that combines the two Gospel stories?

To whom does the traditional children's Christmas pageant offer a blessing? If the missing information were added, would it still be a blessing?

As time allows (or as an additional activity), ask each of the two groups to create a children's Christmas pageant script that reflects only the information and events actually found in their assigned Gospel.

A "NORMAL" CHRISTMAS

Leader preparation: Perhaps no other tradition is as potentially meaningful, or as potentially ingrown, as the family Christmas celebration. Each family, it seems, has unwritten and unspoken "rules" about everything—from the food that's served and who makes it, to how gift wrap is disposed of. There are informal ceremonies of welcome, gift giving, present opening, and departure. Changes in these ceremonies can create gentle awkwardness at best, and deep woundedness, at worst. This activity encourages young adults to name some of these traditions and practice compromising and synchronizing traditions so that everyone is blessed.

Supplies:

- markers and newsprint
- (optional) recorded instrumental Christmas music and device to play it

As the group gathers, encourage everyone to think about his or her family's Christmas celebration. Tell them they will be asked to talk about the traditions that are most important or meaningful to them. Allow some quiet time (perhaps with some instrumental Christmas music playing in the background) for thought.

Invite the group to plan a Christmas celebration that includes all of their families' traditions. To make this easier, separate the preparation for Christmas from the actual Christmas-day activities. On one piece of newsprint, print "Getting Ready," and then solicit traditions related to preparing for the Christmas activities. Topics to include:

Who gets presents, who buys them, and why?

When do we get together (day and time) and why?

What do we cook, who cooks it, and why?

What decorations do we put up and why?

On another piece of newsprint, print "The Event," and then solicit traditions related to the actual Christmas celebration. Topics to include:

Is the day organized or chaotic and why?

What is the schedule or agenda and why?

Does the schedule or agenda involve religious activities? Why or why not?

How do we open presents and why?

Have the group work together to imagine a single common tradition through which everyone in the group would be blessed.

HAVING AN EPIPHANY?

Leader preparation: This activity focuses on Epiphany, an important historical event in the life of Jesus and the Jewish people. In the church's liturgy, Epiphany (the first day after the twelve days of Christmas) represents a change in the way God shared God's message of love, reconciliation, and redemption with the world. Epiphany represents God's decision to send God's Son to speak to the Gentiles, not just to the Jews. Personally, we may use the word "epiphany" to describe a personal "a-ha!" moment, a discovery of something we didn't know or understand before. In our faith journey, this discovery represents the "unveiling" of the truth to help us in our journey. This is why keeping a journal can be helpful. Sometimes, little epiphanies that happen at different times can join together and provide a big epiphany.

Supplies:

- Bible (any translation)
- pen/paper

Invite someone to read Matthew 2:13–16. Pause for a moment for all to process what they heard and for them to write some ideas/thoughts on paper or in their journals. Ask someone to volunteer to lead the discussion. Ask each person to share one thought about or response to this story:

What feeling does this story bring to your mind?

Does it seem fair or just that innocent children are killed because Herod was deceived by the Magi?

Where is justice in this story?

How do you think God felt about this massacre?

What is going on in our world that might be equivalent to the "massacre of the innocents"?

What might we do about it?

When all have shared their thoughts, talk with one another about how this part of the birth story of Jesus impacts the way we think about Christmas. Conclude this activity by asking someone to pray for everyone to have a better understanding of the meaning of Christmas, the importance of Epiphany in understanding the story of God's people, and an understanding of our responsibility to stand up to such violence.

ACTIVITIES FOR
YOUTH
(AGES 12-17)

These Advent and Christmas activities will foster faith development while bringing youth of all ages together in a nurturing team environment.

LAS POSADAS

Leader preparation: This is a Mexican Christmas tradition. Please read the following description of *Las Posadas*. This activity could be reenacted, if desired. If you have members who participate in *Las Posadas*, invite them to share their experience so you can learn more about their tradition.

Supplies:

- costumes or pieces from a nativity set
- (optional) piñata

Las Posadas is celebrated in Mexico and other Spanish-speaking countries from December 16–24, the nine days before Christmas. It is an enactment of Mary and Joseph's struggle to find lodging. Ask children, youth, and adults to gather at dusk, holding candles. Have nine families agree to be innkeepers. Either sculptures of Joseph and Mary riding a donkey are carried in a procession or live characters perform those roles. The travelers follow. For eight evenings, the procession and travelers knock at an innkeeper's door and each night they are not allowed entrance. Everyone returns home disappointed.

On the ninth evening, the innkeeper welcomes Mary, Joseph, the donkey, and the travelers. There is a celebration. Prayers are recited around the inn's nativity scene, carols are sung, a feast is enjoyed, and there is a piñata for the children filled with candy and small toys. The evening ends with a candle-lit procession to the church for the Christmas Eve service.

During these nine days, encourage participants to reflect on times when they haven't recognized the Holy in their presence. Ask them to be alert for signs of the Holy this week in their interactions. How do they recognize the Holy One in their midst?

PRESENCE

Leader preparation: This activity is about *presents* and *presence*. Help participants understand that the whole gift-giving-getting thing is more than lists and shopping. Remind your participants to think beyond themselves.

Supplies:

- markers
- scissors
- card stock
- string or ribbon

The Magi traveled from very far away to bring gifts to the Christ child. Invite the participants to make a gift tag like they would find on any Christmas present, including details like borders and decorations. On the tag write "To: God" and "From: [participant's name]." Discuss what gifts we give to God. Is it like trying to buy a present for the person who has everything? What does God want for Christmas? The point of this activity is to suggest that what God wants from us is to see us use and share the gifts we have been given. Provide plenty of time for reflection on this strategic stewardship/discipleship question.

THE SOUND OF ONE HAND WRAPPING

Leader preparation: Sometimes it's easier to talk with someone whose hands are busy. You don't have to wait until the activity is over to start the discussion.

Supplies:
- boxes
- tape
- scissors
- Christmas wrapping paper

This activity is mostly for "grins," but you can get a good discussion out of it. Divide your group into pairs or trios and invite them to wrap up the box you've supplied like a Christmas present. The "catch" is that everyone must put their non-dominant hand behind his or her back. Try this as a timed activity, or judge who has the prettiest package. Although it is not really about competition, this can add some fun and keep the event from getting out of hand.

Afterward, gather your group and talk about gifts. (You could also do this while they are working on their wrapping.)

What was the best gift you ever received?

What was the best gift you ever gave?

What gift did you want so badly that you could not imagine not getting it?

What gifts have we been given—globally?

What if God gave you a gift that was the wrong size?

What gifts have you been given by God?

Would you ever return them?

TRADITION. . .OR HABIT?

Leader preparation: "Tradition" comes from the Latin word for "handing over, passing on," and so traditions are beliefs or customs that usually have been taught by one generation to the next, and then to the next, and then to the next, usually by word of mouth or by practice. Traditions are a source of comfort in their consistency throughout time, particularly in moments of uncertainty and insecurity. However, it is said that the words, "We've always done it like this before" are the seven deadliest words in the church! Traditions can lose their meaning and, therefore, their impact, by becoming habits. (Habits are defined as actions that are repeated automatically without much thought or awareness.) This activity challenges the youth to consider the traditions and habits in their lives and within their church, and to think about returning some habits to tradition by remembering their meaning.

Supplies:

- newsprint or white board
- markers

Define "traditions" and "habits" to make the distinction between them. If necessary, give examples of each. Invite the group to think about an "average" day in their life. On the newsprint or white board create two lists: one list of traditions (e.g., eating dinner as a family) and one list of habits (e.g., brushing teeth). Discuss how important the traditions are for the group. Discuss how habits are automatic and don't take much serious thinking.

On a separate piece of newsprint, create a list of traditions in the congregation (e.g., changing the paraments or banners to match the seasons, Christmas Eve worship with candlelight, etc.). Review the list and discuss how important these are for the church and why. Discuss how some of these traditions may have lost meaning or purpose, and that over time, people may have even forgotten why they are done.

CHRISTMAS STEWARDSHIP: MATTHEW 2:1–11

Leader preparation: Read over this activity before the group begins. It probably contains more content and group exercises than you can use. So please review it before the group meets and customize it for your participants. If you do not edit this activity, you will need 45–60 minutes to complete all of it.

Supplies:

- Bibles
- hymnals
- a nativity (crèche) with Magi
- a CD player
- CDs of several popular Christmas songs, including "Santa Baby" (Eartha Kitt), "All I Want for Christmas Is You" (Mariah Carey), "The Twelve Days of Christmas," and "The Little Drummer Boy."

Begin by asking the group if they ever think about Christmas, or if they ever sing Christmas music at times other than Advent or Christmas. Set up the nativity set or crèche and ask: Have you ever wondered why we celebrate Christmas only in December? If Christmas is a holiday of great joy, shouldn't we celebrate it more often?

Tell the group that we learn a lot about stewardship, both positively and negatively, from our Christmas traditions and music, and from the Christmas story itself. Play one or more secular Christmas songs that emphasize Christmas as a season for gift-giving and gift-receiving ("Santa Baby" and "The Twelve Days of Christmas" may be among the most blatant of such songs). After playing the song(s), ask the group: What do these songs tell us about stewardship and about Christmas? The group may offer several responses. For example:

- Some songs tell us that Christmas is about gift-giving and materialism.
- Some tell us that it's better to receive than it is to give.

- Some of the songs tell us that relationships are more important than gifts (but that gifts are nice, too).
- Many of these songs convey the idea that what's important is not the monetary value of the gift ("Santa Baby" aside), but the act of giving itself.

Ask someone in the group to read Matthew 2:1–11. Identify the Magi in the crèche and encourage group discussion around the question of what the arrival of the Magi, and this passage in particular, tells us about the Christmas story. Ask: What, if anything, do these verses tell us about stewardship? The most important gifts the Magi brought to the Christ Child were not the material gifts, but first, their gifts of time, energy, and abilities, after having embarked on a very uncertain journey—and second, their gift of worship.

Even Herod and his chief priests and teachers had stewardship roles to fulfill—they helped to advance the Christmas story—despite Herod's many fears and his jealousies. Note that Herod was frightened by the birth of Jesus because he saw Jesus as a potential rival king. Although Herod harbored these negative feelings toward Jesus, God used him to help the Magi in their quest. Herod and the Magi saw each other as strangers and may have been suspicious of each other's intentions and good will. (Explain that this fear of and hostility toward strangers is called xenophobia. We see a lot of xenophobia played out in the United States and in the world today.) Ask: Who or what groups of people today are like Herod? Who celebrates Christmas for what we might consider to be "the wrong reasons" or "negative" motives? Examples might include merchants and shop owners for whom Christmas is a season of nonstop selling and "getting into the black" financially; family members and friends who see Christmas only as a sentimental holiday of partying, decorating, and gift-giving and receiving—and who seem to miss the "real meaning" of Christmas; anyone who doesn't seem to think of Christmas, or celebrate it, the way we do.

Emphasize that one of the great lessons of this story is that it's difficult to judge the motives of other people, or to call other people hypocrites, because we don't know what's in their hearts. We, too, can be xenophobic! Even those who look different or are different from us, even those who think and act differently from us, can help and guide us—whether we're celebrating Christmas, worshiping God, or learning how to fix a flat tire or bake a cake. Conclude this activity by playing "The Little Drummer Boy."

BETHLEHEM: THE WORD BECAME FLESH

Leader preparation: This activity is effective during any season. If you are unable to locate a manger, create one from tri-folded paper so that the paper remains upright. Add some grass or sand in front, and the youth can imagine the rest. If you have youth who are new to the Christian faith and who may not have a manger image to recall, print one or find the Christmas expert in your congregation who knows where everything is stored. You may place more than one manger around the room, so more than one person can "visit" Bethlehem.

Supplies:

- manger with baby Jesus or empty manger
- chair
- A manger is a trough for feeding livestock, such as pigs. In the John passage, "the Word became flesh and lived among us." The Word became flesh, was wrapped in swaddling clothes by poor parents, and laid in a manger. Give the sojourners time to travel in their imagination to the manger and to sit with Jesus.

How do you adore this baby?

What are your expectations of this baby?

What can this baby expect from you?

What gifts do you have to give to Jesus?

LIGHT UP THE HOUSE

Leader preparation: Obtain a foam craft ring, evergreen clippings, and candles. Use the color of candles your congregation uses for Advent. Some congregations use all purple candles, some all blue, and some use three purple or three blue and one pink.

Supplies:

- Bibles
- foam craft ring
- evergreen clippings
- (optional) pine cones, ribbon, holly clippings
- one white pillar candle
- four taper candles: purple, blue, or three purple or three blue and one pink
- glue
- lighter or matches
- candle snuffer

Lighting candles at Advent is a common tradition in the life of the church. Provide the supplies needed for the group to create their own Advent wreath. A foam craft ring forms the foundation with evergreen clippings covering it. Candles may be pressed into the form at four equally separated points. Other items such as ribbons, holly, or pine cones can be added as well. The students might even add some creative decorations of their own invention. Use glue to secure any decorations that will not stick firmly in the craft foam. Candles may also be secured in the foam using glue. The white pillar candle is placed in the center of the wreath. It is the Christ candle. Once the wreath is completed, gather around the wreath and invite volunteers to read the following scriptures while other volunteers light each candle at the appropriate time. At the end, give thanks for Christ's presence with us all year long. Extinguish the candle.

- Candle 1, Hope (Isaiah 60:2–3)
- Candle 2, Peace (Mark 1:2–3)
- Candle 3, Joy (Isaiah 35:10)
- Candle 4, Love (Isaiah 9:6–7)
- White Christ Candle

ACTIVITIES FOR
OLDER
CHILDREN
(AGES 7-11)

The following activities will invite older children to participate more fully in the life of the church by exploring significant Advent and Christmas rituals and traditions.

GIFTS FOR THE BABY

Leader preparation: If you have access to a nativity scene (crèche), bring the figures of the wise ones (Magi), camels, Mary, Joseph, and the baby Jesus to share with your group. If not, find a teaching picture or several old Christmas cards portraying the journey to Bethlehem and the Magi from the east offering gifts to the baby. Read Matthew 2:1–11. Know the story well enough to help the children retell it using the crèche figures or pictures. For this activity, focus on the Magi's gifts as a generous response to God's gift of the child who would be the leader they all awaited, rather than the symbolic nature of the gifts. If the children are curious about the gifts, explain that they were all expensive—gold and fragrant oils and ointments. In Matthew's account, the Magi came from the "east," which could have meant Persia (Iran), Iraq, or Arabia. In any case, they would have had to travel across the Jordanian desert, take the King's Highway (the oldest highway in the world in continuous use) north, possibly stopping in Petra. They may have crossed the Jordan River north of the Dead Sea and gone through Jericho up to Jerusalem to ask King Herod for directions. Bethlehem would have been about six miles from the city. If you would like to see pictures of these areas (for example, the Wadi Rum desert and Petra), go to visitjordan.com, the official website of The Jordan Tourism Board. Some of the rocks in the desert have ancient picture writings left by the many caravans that went through there, so it was a well-traveled route.

Supplies:

- Bible
- nativity figures or pictures of the Magi

Comment that the arrival of a new baby is a special time in a family. If you're a parent, share the gratitude you felt for your new baby, and the way other family members and friends brought gifts when they came to visit the child. Children who have younger brothers or sisters may also have memories about their births to share. Then call attention to the nativity figures (or pictures) and explain that this was what happened when Jesus was born, too. Mary and Joseph looked upon this little boy as a gift from God. They began to realize what a special gift he was when angels sent shepherds to see him and strangers, following a star, from far away, came to bring him presents. Ask the children to tell what they know about these strangers and fill in the details as necessary. Conclude with something like this: The Magi knew Jesus was God's most precious gift to us, and they brought the best of what they had as gifts to honor and welcome him. Because Jesus is the best of all the blessings God has given us, we, too, bring him gifts. (Because the story is so familiar, you might invite the children to tell it as you hold up the figures in the nativity or point to them in the picture.)

A CHILDREN'S CHOIR AND STEWARDSHIP

Leader preparation: Prepare to tell this true story about how a children's choir got involved in a stewardship project.

Supplies:
- newsprint or white board
- markers

Every year the children's choir went Christmas caroling at the homes of older church members and shut-ins. They sang a few carols and left a small box of homemade cookies at each home. One of their regular stops was at the home of Bill, an older man who lived alone in a rooming house above a downtown store. As the children climbed the steep stairway to find his room, they noticed the dingy, dark halls and the lone bathroom at the end of the hall. When they knocked on Bill's door and started singing for him, other men came out in the hall to listen and looked longingly at the box of cookies they left. The children wished they had brought more cookies. So the next year when they caroled for Bill, they brought extra boxes for these men, too. They were all men who, for one reason or another, lived alone in this dreary place without friends or family. The children thought how hard it must be for them at Christmas, so the next year they made Christmas stockings out of paper bags for them, and filled the stockings with small gifts as well as cookies. The men greeted them with smiles.

Later, back at the church, one of the older girls in the choir had an idea. "Let's ask our parents to help us cook dinner here at the church for the men who live above the store. We'll ask Bill to invite them." The choir children and their parents began making plans. On the day of the dinner, they cooked the food together, set a beautiful table, and waited for their guests. Imagine their disappointment when only one man came: Bill. As they sat down to eat together, Bill explained that the men in the rooming house didn't go to any church, and they were afraid to come with him. They didn't think they had proper clothes, and they weren't sure they would know how to act in a church. The children and their parents looked at one another. They looked at all the food they had prepared, and then someone said, "Well then, why don't we take our dinner to them?"

And that's just what they did. They found containers in the kitchen, packed up a dinner for each man, and took it to the rooming house. The men were happy to have the meals, and took them back into their rooms to eat. The children returned to the church with their parents a little wiser, but happy, too, that they had found a way to share their meal after all.

Tell the children this true story, and then ask: What can we learn from the experiences these children had with stewardship? Write their responses in simple words on the chart or board.

Then pray: "God, whose giving knows no ending, help us to keep all we have learned in our minds and hearts as we plan our own giving projects as stewards of your love. Amen."

CELEBRATING THE SEASONS

Leader preparation: The church year is filled with celebrations in which we bring out our best and dress up our worship. Many churches decorate with banners and flowers at Christmas and Easter, but at what other times in the church year can we bring out the beauty of the season and enhance our space? If possible, talk with the person in charge of your worship space and ask if your group can plan to prepare the space in a special way for one of the upcoming Sundays.

Supplies:
- markers and newsprint or whiteboard
- "Seasons of the Church Year," page 49
- Bible
- Ask the children to list some seasons of the church year; refer to "Seasons of the Church Year," page 49.

If your church has altar cloths, talk about the different colors of the cloths that are used for each season and what symbols they might have on them. Do people order special flowers for certain days or times of the year? Are banners hung in your sanctuary for certain occasions?

What other decorations do you remember using at different times of the church year? Think about the coming Sundays. Is there a Sunday on which your group would like to prepare the worship space in a special way?

Invite the children to create a paper banner that could form the basis for the development of a cloth banner. These questions may help guide your project:

In what season of the church year will this Sunday fall?

What scripture will you feature? (If your pastor follows the Revised Common Lectionary, ask which texts will be used on the Sunday you've chosen.)

What colors will you use? Why?

What images would you want on the banner? How will those images help the congregation understand the worship theme that day?

Option: If there are people in your congregation who sew, see if they would be willing to create a cloth banner from the children's paper banner.

SEASONS OF THE CHURCH YEAR

SEASON	COLOR	LENGTH
Advent	Blue/Purple	4 weeks before Dec. 25
Christmas	White	12 days
Epiphany	White or Green	7-9 weeks, depends on the date of Easter
Lent	Purple	6 weeks
Easter/Eastertide	White/Gold	50 days
Pentecost Day	Red	1 Sunday
Season after Pentecost, or Ordinary Time	Green	After Pentecost until Advent

SOME SPECIAL DAYS TO CONSIDER DURING THESE SEASONS:

Advent
Blue Christmas service (Resources can be found on Google by searching for "Blue Christmas Service.")

Epiphany
Baptism of Jesus
   (first Sunday after Epiphany)
Transfiguration
   (last Sunday after Epiphany)

Lent
Ash Wednesday
Palm Sunday/Passion Sunday
Holy Thursday (Maundy Thursday)
Good Friday

Easter

Season After Pentecost
Pentecost Sunday
Trinity Sunday
   (first Sunday after Pentecost)
World Communion Sunday
   (first Sunday in October)
Reign of Christ Sunday
   (last Sunday after Pentecost)

SOME OTHER DATES TO CONSIDER
(Check with your denomination to see when these are celebrated and what resources are available.)

New Year's Day (Some churches have a special celebration on this day.)

Martin Luther King Jr. Day
   (or closest Sunday)

Health and Human Service Sunday

Racial Justice Sunday

Church Vocations Sunday

Amistad Sunday

Pacific Islander and Asian American
   Ministries Sunday

Mother's Day

Father's Day

Christian Education Sunday

American Indian Ministry Sunday

Access and Disabilities Sunday

Children's Sabbath

Higher Education Sunday

Laity Sunday

Stewardship Sunday

LAS POSADAS—ROOM AT THE INN

Leader preparation: In Hispanic communities, the nine days leading up to Christmas form the season of *Las Posadas*. In this activity, learners will experience *Las Posadas* and make discoveries about hospitality and welcoming the strangers in our midst. You will need to prepare stations in your learning space or around your sanctuary for this activity. Mark out the stopping points with a cross on a piece of paper. The number of stations depends on the size of your space and the number of children participating. Try to have at least three or four places. Alternatively, provide two simple costumes for Mary and Joseph and similar simple stoles for the innkeepers. In a separate location and possibly outside, arrange a station for the ninth night and the piñata party.

The festive process of *Las Posadas* moves from inside the church out into the street and neighborhoods. Children and adults take turns each night, some playing Joseph and Mary and some playing the innkeepers with no room for the tired couple. At each stop or station on the walk, those playing the role of Joseph stop and knock. At the first stop, Joseph says in a loud voice, "In the name of heaven, good innkeeper, do you have shelter for us tonight?" The innkeeper says, "This is not an inn; move on. I cannot open lest you be a scoundrel." At each stop the innkeeper becomes angry at the knock on the door and rude in his or her refusal of Joseph's request. Finally, at the last stop, Joseph tells the innkeepers that he needs *posada* or shelter, even for just one night, for his wife, who is the Queen of Heaven. No one will let them in until the ninth night, which is Christmas Eve. Then Joseph's request is met with love by an innkeeper who gives the young couple permission to stay in his stable. All the participants celebrate the generosity of the innkeeper and the shelter given to Mary and Joseph. The celebration includes dancing, music, food, and drinks. For the children there is a piñata with candy and other treats. The festival reminds everyone to be ready, for the stranger who comes to the door just might be God or Jesus in disguise.

Supplies:

- simple costumes for Mary and Joseph
- simple earth-colored fabric remnants that could be worn as a stole by those playing innkeepers; enough stoles so that an innkeeper at each stop can wear one
- a piñata in the shape of a star or other Christmas symbol
- candy, pennies, or small trinkets to fill the piñata
- a stick and blindfold for breaking the piñata
- small bags for the children to collect their treats from the piñata
- Latin American or Hispanic Christmas music
- music player

Explain to the learners that they will experience an Advent festival conducted in Latin American communities in the United States and Mexico. Show them where Mexico is on your globe or wall map. Remember to ask and see if any of your learners participate in or have had an experience of *Las Posadas*, and invite them to share their experience. Otherwise, share the basic notes listed in the leader preparation section above. Divide the group into Marys, Josephs, and innkeepers. Choose at least one person in each group to wear the simple costume. Ask all who are playing the innkeeper to move to the various spots except for the station with the piñata. Move the Mary and Joseph group to the beginning of the route. Let the procession begin. At each station, Joseph knocks and asks for shelter for Mary and himself. Each time, the innkeepers tell them they have no room and to move on. Have the whole group move through the three or four stations simulating the parade of the first eight nights of the festival.

Reassemble all the learners and send some to the piñata station to be innkeepers. Mix up your Marys and Josephs so other learners have a chance to participate. (There's no rule that only girls can be Mary and boys can be Joseph.) Then set off in a weary, slow walk. When the children reach the station with the piñata, have Joseph knock and ask his line very wearily. The innkeepers throw open the door and greet the couple with joy. Turn on some music to create a fiesta-like atmosphere and let the children take turns with the piñata. After it breaks and everything is collected, invite the learners to relax and have a conversation about what it felt like to be Mary and Joseph, to be refused shelter, and what it was like to gain it in the end. Ask them if they know or can name people without shelter in their community. In Mark 9:33–37 we are reminded that whoever welcomes the least also welcomes Jesus. Conclude with a prayer of thanksgiving for shelter and a prayer for care for those in the community in need of housing and hope.

CELEBRATING THE BIRTH OF CHRIST IN INDIA

Leader preparation: This activity could take up an entire session. To condense the activity you may wish to make the star ornament, share the Christmas greeting, and read the scripture text. If you include food in the session, be sensitive to allergies. Prepare the food ahead of time. If you are unable to make the Indian foods listed in this activity, provide cookies, fruit, and punch or cider. Many of the foods we eat at Christmas are also enjoyed in India. For the star craft, prepare the star shapes with the hot glue gun ahead of time, and then let the children decorate them in the session. Depending on the amount of time you have allotted for this activity, you may decorate your learning space with lights and candles as simply or elaborately as you wish. Enjoy the food after the reading of the nativity scripture to simulate the feasts held after midnight Mass in India. It will be helpful to note with learners that India is a vast country and so there are many different traditions depending on the state or geographic region. Although this activity is focused on Christmas, it can be enjoyed year round.

Background: There have been Christians in India since the first century of the Common Era. Some believe that the disciple Thomas traveled to India after the crucifixion of Jesus and arrived in Malabar in 52 CE. Today there are an estimated 24 million Christians in India, making it the third largest religion in the country. This long history yields rich traditions and theology only recently appreciated in the West. Many Indians, Christian or not, celebrate Christmas. People walk in family groups to their churches on December 24. The churches are decorated with poinsettias and candles. After, there are feasts of curries and other dishes. Christian homes display nativity scenes in their front windows and there are sometimes competitions for the best scene. In place of evergreen trees or wreaths, many people will decorate with mango leaves. People string up giant paper lanterns shaped like stars between houses to commemorate the star that heralded Jesus' birth in Bethlehem. In Southern India, little clay lamps are placed outside to show that Jesus is the light of world. On Christmas day, school children perform nativity plays followed by the singing of carols and eating sweets. Then Father Christmas comes with presents. He is called "Christmas Baba" in the Hindi language and "Christmas Thaathaa" in Tamil. Christmas caroling parties go on the whole week before and after Christmas as people sing the story of the faith in their neighborhoods.

Christmas day is called "Bada Din" in Hindi, which means "Big Day." It is a national holiday in India.

Supplies:

- map of India
- nativity scene
- Bible in a child-friendly translation, with Luke 2:1–20 bookmarked
- Christmas lights
- votive candles
- recordings of Christmas carols and a music player
- traditional Indian food: See Indian food recipes on pages 54 and 55
- star ornament: See "Make a Five-Pointed Star" activity on page 56
- fruit punch or other juice
- (optional) Indian Christmas songs: Hindi Christmas songs with English subtitles; found on YouTube
- (optional) images of walking to midnight Mass in India on star lantern-lined streets

Welcome the children to the festival. Have music playing and the room partially decorated for Christmas. Share with children the basic notes in the leader preparation section. Show them where India is located on the map or globe. Invite them to make a star ornament. As they finish making their decorations, hang the decorations around the learning space to dry. Work together to set up the nativity scene. Gather around the scene and read the account of Christ's birth in Luke 2:1–20. You may wish to pass the Bible around so each child can read a part of the story in scripture. Divide the group into two sides. Have one side stand up, turn to the others, and shout in happy voices, "Merry, Merry Christmas." Then have the other side also stand, turn to the first side, and say, "Happy, Happy, Christmas." Repeat this several times and encourage the children to be loud. This greeting is given with great joy in India. Enjoy sweets and sing carols. Conclude the session with another round of the Merry Christmas greeting.

SAFFRON/CARDAMOM BUNS

Ingredients:

2 1/8 c. milk, warmed slightly

½ tsp salt

1 ½ c. sour cream

2/3 c. sugar

7½ cups all-purpose flour

½ c. butter

2 ½ tsp compressed fresh yeast

¼ tsp powdered saffron or ½ tsp powdered cardamom

1 beaten egg

1 cup raisins (optional)

Directions:

- Heat milk and butter in a small saucepan until butter melts and the temperature reaches 100 degrees.
- Crumble the yeast into a bowl, and then pour in the warm milk. Stir well until the yeast dissolves.
- Prepare dough by mixing sour cream, powdered saffron or powdered cardamom, sugar, salt, and 7 cups of flour all together in a bowl.
- Cover and set aside for 40 minutes.
- Prepare two or three baking sheets by covering each with a sheet of parchment paper.
- Now divide the dough into 35 pieces and roll each piece into a 6-inch rope. With the rope lying flat on the work surface, roll each end toward the center, in opposite directions, creating a curled "S" shape.
- Place the buns on the prepared baking sheets and garnish with raisins, if desired. Cover with a towel, let rise, and bake in a preheated oven at 425 degrees for about 10 minutes.
- Cool 5 minutes before eating.

TURKISH DELIGHT

Ingredients:

2 cups granulated sugar

1¼ cups water

1 lemon, the peel cut into strips, the juice squeezed

1 orange, the peel cut into strips, the juice squeezed

4 tablespoons unflavored powdered gelatin

2 tablespoons confectioners' sugar

1 tablespoon cornstarch

Directions:

- Dissolve the granulated sugar in half of the water over medium heat.
- Add the strips of lemon and orange peel and the juices. Bring the mixture to a boil and simmer for 15 minutes.
- Soften the gelatin by soaking it for 5–10 minutes in the rest of the water. Add the gelatin to the sugar syrup stirring well, and boil for 10 minutes, until the syrup reaches the thread stage.
- Strain the mixture into a shallow dampened pan or onto platters, and let it set for 24 hours.
- Cut the candy into 1-inch squares.
- Sift the confectioners' sugar and cornstarch together into a shallow dish. Roll the pieces of candy in the mixture.
- Store the squares in boxes with more confectioners' sugar and cornstarch between each layer.

MAKE A FIVE-POINTED STAR

Supplies:

- craft sticks (either plain or colored; see instructions below for options)
- craft jewels, stones, buttons, or beads
- glitter glue
- hot glue and hot glue gun
- ribbon
- scissors
- (optional) paint brush and paints

Instructions: Make five-pointed stars by hot gluing together the craft sticks. Paint the star in the desired color and let it dry completely. You may use colored craft sticks or plain ones and leave them in the natural wood color to save time. Make a loop of a ribbon and glue it at the back of the star, so that you can hang the star ornament. Glue on beads, buttons, jewels, or other assorted decorative items to decorate the star. Add glitter glue to make some of the stars sparkly.

HOLIDAY RITUALS

Leader preparation: What are the different rituals that your church observes around Advent and Christmas, Lent and Easter, and other holidays? What items would serve as reminders of each of these rituals? If you are doing this activity at the time of year of a particular holiday, you may want to focus more on those particular rituals. Gather supplies and place them in a box or bag to keep them out of sight.

Supplies:
- items that will remind the group of special holiday rituals, such as a nativity set or Advent candle wreath, an Easter lily or Easter egg, a chrismon, and so forth
- box or bag to place items in
- paper and pencils

Ask your group to think about the different rituals that take place in your church around certain holidays. Focusing on one holiday at a time, bring out the related items one by one. Have someone keep track of the rituals for each holiday.

How do these rituals help us to share the stories of our faith?

In what ways do they help us to understand our faith better?

How can they help us explain our faith to others?

Decorate your space with something from each holiday.

HOLIDAY COLLECTION

Leader preparation: We frequently collect items for food baskets or food pantries during the Thanksgiving and Christmas seasons, but the need can be just as great during other times of the year. These collections can take on the feeling of a ritual, especially if the food is blessed before being delivered. This activity can be done in conjunction with your regular holiday collections or as a new "off season" collection. Coordinate this project with your church's Mission Committee. Perhaps the entire congregation can participate. Decide on an organization that will receive the collected items and for how long your group will be collecting them. Find out if there are any special items needed by the organization you select. Get background information about the organization to share with the children. Arrange for delivery of the donations and have the children help, if possible.

Supplies:

- information about the selected organization
- large boxes or grocery bags
- butcher paper to cover boxes
- tape
- markers, crayons, stickers for decorating
- poster

Tell the children they're going to organize a food drive. Tell them about the organization for which they will be collecting items. Explain what the agency does, whom they help, and the kinds of things that they need. Invite the children to create posters, decorate collection boxes or bags, and write a news item for your church newsletter and an announcement to be used during worship. Make sure they include the pertinent information, such as the purpose of the collection, the organization they are collecting for, when items are needed, and what kinds of items are needed. Have the group place the bags or boxes and posters in prominent areas where all will see them. After the food collection is over, have the children gather up the boxes and bags of donations. Offer up a prayer of thanksgiving to God for those who gave, and ask that those who receive the items will be blessed. If the rest of the congregation participated in this activity, this blessing could take place during the worship service.

Deliver the donations and include the children, if possible.

ACTIVITIES FOR
YOUNGER
CHILDREN
(AGES 3-6)

The fun activities in this chapter will encourage this
young and eager age group to form their faith while
learning about Advent and Christmas.

TRADITIONS

Leader preparation: Think about the traditions that your church uses to mark its worship time and the year. Are these traditions rooted in the Bible? Some traditions have become so routine that they are hard to change, while others can have a great deal of variation.

Supplies:
- Bible
- newsprint or whiteboard
- tape
- markers
- paper
- crayons

Gather the children in your worship/story area. Talk with them about some of the routines they have in their family, such as getting ready for bed at night and getting ready in the morning. Then talk about the ways they celebrate their birthdays. Tell them that routine is a tradition, something their family does every year. Ask them to describe some other traditions in their family, such as Christmas or Easter celebrations. Write their ideas on the newsprint or whiteboard. Show the children the Bible and tell them that our most important church traditions come from the Bible. Talk about showing hospitality, sharing with others, and taking care of others. Let them know that worshipping, praying, and eating together are all things that the Bible tells us we should do. The people who believe in God and Jesus have been doing these things for thousands of years. Make a list of things that happen in your services of worship each week, such as a time of greeting or passing of the peace, lighting of candles, music, prayers, offerings, and communion. Give the children a chance to share their favorite traditions from church or home. If there is time, invite them to draw a picture of them.

A THANK YOU PARTY

Leader preparation: Bring items for a celebration, including decorations and food.

Supplies:
- decorations, such as crepe paper and balloons
- healthy party foods

Invite everyone to imagine it's Christmas morning. They look under the tree and see the very present they wanted more than anything else in the whole world. Invite them to act out their reaction to the present. What would they say to or do for the person who gave them that special gift? Explain that God has given us all the things that we really, truly want, and our reaction should be the same. We should be jumping for joy and shouting, "Thank you!" to God. Help participants plan and carry out a "Thank You Party" to thank God for all the gifts God has given us.

STAR DUST

Leader preparation: Set up a center for making star wands, so that participants can work on this as they arrive. Since the stars may be used during the workshop, avoid decorating them with materials that need to dry. Instead, provide brightly colored markers and/or stickers. Gem stickers, in particular, may add some fun sparkle.

Supplies:
- stars drawn on poster board or card stock
- markers
- brightly colored stickers
- thin dowels or sticks cut into 18" lengths
- ribbon
- scissors
- duct tape
- image of Orion's Nebula, found on Google images

If possible, display an image of Orion's Nebula for inspiration. It shows that stars do not always appear to be gold or silver. Through a telescope, the nebula looks more like a swirling rainbow. When everyone has finished decorating their stars, attach them to a wand-sized dowel with strong tape. For added interest, staple brightly colored ribbons onto the base of the star.

As participants are working on the wands, talk to them about star stuff. Carl Sagan popularized the idea that the earth and all creatures are made up of star stuff. The atoms that eventually became you and me began their life billions of years ago inside a star. Having God inside of us is kind of like knowing that the smallest parts of us are made of star dust. God made us in God's image. We have a divine spark—or "God flame"—inside of us. How do you think God shines out from us?

When wands are finished, have the children wander around the room, holding wands in the air and waving them, creating a swirling night sky.

THE CHURCH YEAR AND CELEBRATION STATIONS: ADVENT, CHRISTMAS, AND EPIPHANY

Leader preparation: The church year provides many opportunities for celebrations and traditions. Young children love celebrations and enjoy marking traditions with activities. Consider the various Advent, Christmas, and Epiphany rituals and celebrations within the liturgical or church year and the way your church celebrates these events. Review "The Church Year." Gather supplies and set up the stations. Decide how you want the children to explore the stations, such as rotating in intervals or wandering as they choose.

Supplies:

- "The Church Year," page 66
- supplies for stations
- (optional) adult helpers

Ask the children which seasonal holidays they enjoy. Tell them the church has seasons and special days, too. Use the talking points on the "The Church Year" to explain the church year to the children, emphasizing Advent, Christmas, and Epiphany. Introduce the celebration stations and invite them to explore them as you've determined.

THE CHURCH YEAR

The church has a calendar that revolves around the life of Jesus. Although the activities in this chapter focus on Advent, Christmas, and Epiphany, an overview of the entire church calendar is given here.

The church calendar begins with the four weeks of **Advent**, which is the time before Christmas when people in the church prepare for the birth of Jesus on Christmas day.

The church calendar continues with the season of **Christmas** to the day of **Epiphany**, January 6, when we celebrate the visit of the wise men.

The church year has two times called **Ordinary Time**, which aren't ordinary at all, but rather, counts the Sundays until the next season. The first Ordinary Time is from Epiphany to the season of Lent. During Ordinary Time we learn about Jesus and his life and teachings.

Lent is a time for prayer and penitence. Penitence is a big word that means, "I'm sorry, God." Lent is the 40 days leading up to Holy Week and Easter.

Holy Week begins with **Palm Sunday**, when Jesus rode into Jerusalem on a donkey and many people greeted him as a king. In the days following, Jesus had his last supper with his disciples, was betrayed by one of them, taken to the courts, was crucified, and died on the cross.

On **Easter** day we celebrate that God raised Jesus from the dead, that he is alive, and that he visited with many of his friends. During the season of Easter we celebrate the resurrection of Jesus and that he sent the Holy Spirit to be with us always.

Pentecost is called "the birthday of the church" because that's the day the Holy Spirit came upon the disciples and many others in Jerusalem. Jesus' disciples started to preach and teach, and others wanted to be followers of Jesus. This was how the church began long, long ago.

After Pentecost is another season of Ordinary Time, counting the Sundays until we are back to Advent.

CELEBRATION STATIONS: SPOTLIGHT ON ADVENT, CHRISTMAS, AND EPIPHANY

Set up stations in your space for Advent, Christmas, and Epiphany. Each station offers two activities. Use one or both, or substitute with an activity of your choice that's significant to your church or community. Add décor and symbols at each station to enhance the theme. Suggestions are given, but use your own creativity and available supplies as well. You will need an adult helper at each station to guide the children as they explore that station.

ADVENT CELEBRATION STATION

Display Suggestions: Advent wreath, Advent banners, Advent calendar, purple or blue fabric (liturgical color for Advent)

Wait a Minute

You'll need a stopwatch or way to time exactly one minute. Begin by telling the children that Advent is a season of waiting—waiting for Christmas. This can be hard, just like waiting for anything for very long is hard. Tell the children they are going to play a game called "Wait a Minute." Invite them all to stand and stay standing for however long they think that a minute really is (which you'll actually be timing). Tell them they can sit down at whatever point they think has been a minute. Remind them that a minute is probably going to be longer than they think. Remind them to decide for themselves, rather than doing what other children might be doing. At the end of the minute (slightly past), announce the end of the time and the names of those who were closest to the minute mark.

Sing a Song of Advent (tune: "Twinkle, Twinkle Little Star"):

Advent is a time to wait,

Not quite time to celebrate.

Light the candles one by one,

Till the Advent time is done.

Christmas Day will soon be here,

Time for joy, and time for cheer!

CHRISTMAS CELEBRATION STATION

Display Suggestions: Nativity set, angels, a Christmas tree, some chrismons, music player playing Christmas music

Wrap Up a Baby

Provide various sizes and types of baby dolls and blankets or pieces of cloth. Demonstrate various ways to wrap a baby in a blanket, which might include what swaddling clothes would have been like. Invite the children to take turns wrapping up "baby Jesus." Provide as many dolls and wraps as possible, so many children can do this at once.

Away in a Manger (with suggested motions)

Away in a manger,

(hold arms like holding baby—could even be the baby dolls from previous activity—and rock the baby back and forth)

No crib for his bed,

(continue rocking baby, but shake head "no" on word "no")

The little lord Jesus

Laid down his sweet head;

(place two hands together and place them under head, tilted to one side or other)

The stars in the heavens

(point up to the stars in the sky)

Looked down where he lay,

(point downward and look down)

The little Lord Jesus

Asleep on the hay.

(lay head on hands again and sway back and forth in rocking motion)

EPIPHANY CELEBRATION STATION

Display Suggestions: Nativity set. Especially focus on the kings/wise men. If possible, have many different depictions of pictures and figures of the wise men, stars hanging around (especially a big one lit up), incense burning or scented candle, and either real gold, frankincense, and myrrh or things to represent such gifts.

Dress Like Kings

Provide various crowns (paper or play ones) and kings' costumes and robes for a time of dress-up play. You could perhaps make a relay race out of taking turns dressing in the king's clothes.

Making Stars

Make a simple star craft out of paper, felt, or foam.

ACTIVITIES FOR
INTERGENERATIONAL
GROUPS

The following Advent and Christmas activities will
accommodate the broad spectrum of faith development
and life experiences in this all-ages group.

CHRISTMAS:
THE WORD BECAME FLESH

Leader preparation: Regardless of the season, display a nativity set. "The Word became flesh and lived among us" is an eight-word summary of Jesus from John 1. Celebrate the Word coming to us as a baby in Bethlehem.

Supplies:

- nativity set
- Christmas snack (perhaps tangerines or shortbread cookies)
- recordings of Christmas carols and sound equipment
- Bible

Ask an older learner to find John 1 and read aloud verses 1 and 14 (or read the verses yourself). In the Gospel of John we hear that "the Word became flesh and lived among us." "Became flesh" means became a living person. Who do you think this person is that is being described? What do you think the author is saying about who Jesus is? What would it mean for a word to come alive?

Invite the group to set up the nativity set and talk together about Jesus' birth. What do you remember about the Christmas story? Conclude with a Christmas snack. Play Christmas carols as you eat.

HOLY LINENS

Leader preparation: Paraments are the cloths that cover the pulpit, Bible, and communion table or altar. Make sure that either the sanctuary or storage area where paraments or banners are kept is available for the group to explore.

Centering Prayer: Artful Weaver, help me feel your delight at all of the brightly colored threads that pattern your world. Help me trust in your vision for beautiful designs that are unfolding. Where threads have broken, guide all your people toward healing practices that honor the hurt places and that open our eyes to new beauty that may emerge from them. Amen.

Supplies:

- Bible
- (optional) someone in your church who helps care for the paraments and can answer the group's questions
- (optional) a collection of yarn including the colors blue, purple, and red

Ask the group to listen closely to the scripture reading, paying special attention to what both men and women brought and what the women donated on their own. Read Exodus 35:20–29. If available, spread out a variety of yarn, and have the children pick out the colors of yarn the women spun. Talk about how these colors are used in your own church in different seasons of the church year, such as Advent, Christmas, Lent, Easter, and Pentecost. Typically, blue and purple are the "getting ready" colors used during Advent and Lent in anticipation of Christmas and Easter. White symbolizes the new life of Jesus' resurrection. Red symbolizes the fire of the Holy Spirit during Pentecost. Green symbolizes the Ordinary Time of daily ministry.

ACTIVITIES FOR
SEEKERS AND THOSE
NEW TO CHURCH

These activities are designed to welcome adults and
youth with little or no experience in a faith community
to learn about and embrace some of the church's
significant Advent and Christmas practices.

CELTIC HIGH CROSSES

Leader preparation: Familiarize yourself with Celtic High Crosses, in particular, St. Martin's Cross. You can learn about these crosses from Wikipedia, and images can be found on Google Images. Locate a picture of St. Martin's Cross and one of a Celtic High Cross that contains an image of the birth story to show the group. Set up a computer and data projector. Read the birth narratives in Luke and Matthew.

Supplies:

- newsprint or a whiteboard
- markers
- Internet access and data projector
- Bibles
- self-hardening clay or modeling compound, cut into rectangular blocks
- carving implements such as kitchen knives, toothpicks, and small chisels

One ancient Christian tradition is the Celtic High Cross. Celtic Christianity had its beginnings with St. Patrick from 4th century Ireland. From Ireland, Christianity spread to Scotland. It is from Ireland and Iona that the use of Celtic High Crosses sprung up. Display St. Martin's Cross on the projector. It is on the Isle of Iona in Scotland. On one side of the cross are twining vines, said to symbolize the intertwining of heaven and earth. The side of the cross has carvings of stories from the Bible. The carvings were used to teach and remind people of Bible stories much like stained glass windows were used in later centuries to teach people who were unable to read the Bible. In the middle of the cross is a carving of Mary and the baby Jesus. Invite the learners to remember the story of the birth of Jesus. Ask: How do you recall the birth of Jesus?

As a group, tell the story of Christmas. On newsprint or a whiteboard, record key words (such as "Mary," "Joseph," "angels," "shepherds") that learners will later look up in the Bible. Divide the whole group into four small groups. Invite them to read the birth stories of Jesus in Matthew and Luke using a Bible or online sources (accessed through computers or their smart phones).

What surprised you, if anything? Were there any parts of the story you were unable to find? Why do you think these stories were included in our Bible? Have learners look at the cross with the image of the birth story. Then have them take a block of clay and use carving implements to make a simple image of some part of Jesus' birth story. Give learners time to work, then place the blocks of clay together to make a large cross or crosses. Let the clay harden.

THE OTHER CALENDAR: SPOTLIGHT ON ADVENT AND CHRISTMAS

Leader preparation: Seekers and those new to church may not know anything about the liturgical seasons of the church year; however, it's possible that, aside from Christmas and Easter, many in the pews don't either. The following activities can be shared as open sessions during Advent and Christmas that include longstanding members of the church who wish to know more about when we celebrate, meditate, remember, and tell the stories of our faith. Opening the group sessions to everyone who is interested will not only increase the knowledge base of the community, but also has the potential to begin friendships and establish common ground.

As we move through the liturgical seasons of Advent and Christmas, invite comments from the group about their own practices during these seasons. Create a conversation instead of giving a lecture. Invite stories that help make theses seasons meaningful to the group.

Supplies:

- calendar for the current year
- "The Other Calendar: Spotlight on Advent and Christmas," page 79
- (optional) calendar marking the current liturgical season

Begin by asking people to say words they think of when they hear the word "calendar." We depend on and often appreciate calendars; sometimes we resent their restrictions and reminders of our busy-ness. Most people carry a calendar with them on their cellphone or other electronic device, or have a hard copy in their purse or wallet.

The Christian church also uses a calendar, but it doesn't hang on a wall in the kitchen. It, too, keeps track of birthdays and anniversaries; it reminds us of the holy moments and opportunities to participate and grow in faith. Sometimes we're surprised by what's coming up next when our lives are busy and we're focused on our secular calendar. The liturgical calendar helps us remember our story of faith and worship. Using this calendar of faith, we can tell the story to others and remain faithful in our own lives. By understanding the seasons of the church year, especially Advent and Christmas, which are the focus of this activity, we can live both today and in the grand scope of history and future. Distribute the handout. Walk the group through the seasons of Advent and Christmas. Then invite people to share what they find beautiful about these church seasons.

THE OTHER CALENDAR: SPOTLIGHT ON ADVENT & CHRISTMAS

ADVENT

The season of Advent marks the beginning of the church year. In the four weeks leading up to Christmas, we prepare for the coming of the infant who will change the world. Often the scripture lessons and hymns are anticipatory, looking forward to a time of joy, inviting God to be among us. We prepare ourselves, so that we're ready for the birth. The traditional color for the sanctuary is purple; the modern color is a clear, bright blue (think of the color of Mary's robe in paintings).

- What does this faith community do to keep the season of Advent?

- What other Advent practices do you know about (Advent calendars, Advent candles and wreaths, seasonal music, and so forth)?

CHRISTMAS

Christmas is the season of twelve days that begins at sunset on December 24 and continues through January 6. There are two Sundays of Christmas, simply numbered "the first Sunday of Christmas" and "the second Sunday of Christmas." The season of Christmas celebrates the meeting of the Divine with humanity, when we meet God. Many churches tell the stories of the shepherds (Luke) and the Magi (Matthew) meeting God during this time, too. Also during this season, we hear the story of Jesus' baptism (Mark and John).

- How does this church tell the story during the season of Christmas?

DELIGHTING THE EYE
ADVENT AND CHRISTMAS

Leader preparation: Color is one way we tell our story to ourselves. Check with your worship leaders or pastor to see in what ways your congregation deliberately uses color. Ask if the group might look through the storage closet that contains the paraments, stoles, and banners. If you have time, take a look before the session begins, so you can tailor your conversation to this particular faith community. If the pastor has stoles, ask if you might borrow them or if he/she would like to come to the session to talk about them.

Supplies:

- paraments used within the church community (You may wish to leave them in storage and take the group to see them if possible.)
- stoles from the clergy collection, if available
- fabric or paint color swatches, if paraments and stoles aren't available
- paper
- (optional) colored pencils or markers

The story of faith is told in song, story, and color. Each season of the year uses a color that helps tell its story. The sanctuary is adorned with these colors to help the congregation find beauty, understand the story, and remember the season we are experiencing. For much of the history of Christianity, only a small minority of the faithful were able to read. If the community had a Bible—and many did not—it was not written in the language of the people, but rather in Latin, Greek, or Hebrew. The history of the church, the names and adventures of the faithful of other generations, and the ancient tales of the Old and New Testaments were told in story, mosaic, or stained glass (when there were buildings constructed deliberately as sanctuaries); or in the banners, stoles, and paraments of the season. We continue the tradition of visual narrative today. There are no strict rules about which colors to use. Indeed, traditions around the use of color have changed over the centuries.

The most common liturgical colors used during Advent are violet (purple) and blue.

- **Violet, purple, and black** are the colors of repentance and mourning, and are used for Advent and Lent. Sometimes these colors are also used for funerals or memorial services.

- **Blue** is a modern Advent color that's becoming more common. It is a clear, bright blue like the color of Mary's robe often depicted in paintings.

- **White** indicates purity, and is displayed at Christmas and Easter, as well as for weddings and funerals or memorial services.

- **Gold** is a variant of white, symbolizing the richness of the faithful life.

Invite the group to look at the ways this church uses color during Advent and Christmas. As you move around the sanctuary, take note of the colors in the room: floor, walls, windows, communion table or altar, pews, choir chairs, worship leaders' chairs. Celebrate the gifts of color, texture, and shape in telling the story of faith. Tour the sanctuary to see which colors are teaching the community now. Which colors are permanent (floor and wall coverings, furniture), and which change with the liturgical seasons? Return to your meeting room. Talk about the liturgical seasons with which you are most familiar. What are your favorites? Why?

Option: If your faith community doesn't use banners and paraments or doesn't have a sanctuary, use paper and colored pencils or markers to create some suggested visual lessons for Advent and Christmas.

WORSHIP
RESOURCES FOR
ADVENT AND
CHRISTMAS

These special worship elements infuse scripture,
sacred tradition, and creativity into a meaningful
Advent and Christmas experience your entire
congregation is sure to enjoy.

HANGING OF THE GREENS

Adapted for Children's Message; Engaging the Word; Responding to the Word

Leader preparation: This activity aims to make a connection between stewardship, the ornamentation of Christmas, and the lighting of the Advent wreath. Lighting of the Advent wreath and hanging Christmas greens are beloved traditions in many churches. Meet in advance with various groups in the church to plan for this activity. It could be done all at once or spread out over the seasons of Advent and Christmas. It's an activity that involves smaller groups preparing to present before a larger one.

Supplies:

- an Advent wreath and something to light it
- a sampling of Christmas greens
- a poinsettia
- bells
- a nativity scene
- an ornament with a symbol of Jesus
- a "star" ornament
- poster board and drawing materials

Meet in advance with different groups in your congregation, including study groups, fellowship groups, a faith formation group, a Bible study group, and other established groups. Try to get a variety of age representation. Invite each group to come up with an idea for something to say or do while each Advent candle is being lit. Give each group a theme and a symbol that they can use for each candle and each Sunday. The following chart is an example:

SUNDAY	GROUP	THEME	SYMBOL
Advent 1	Older youth	Hope	Advent wreath
Advent 2	Older adults	Peace	Christmas greens
Advent 3	Older children	Love	Poinsettia
Advent 4	Younger children	Joy	Bells
Christmas Eve	Younger youth	Good news	Nativity scene
Christmas 1	Younger adults	Jesus	Ornament
Christmas 2 or Epiphany 1	Anyone else	Showing Jesus	Star

Some groups might color in the theme of the day on large letters on poster board to raise before the congregation. Allow groups to present their own creative ideas. After each group does its presentation, invite someone to close with a prayer that calls all to care for creation by weaving together the theme and symbol of the day. For instance, for Advent 1, someone might say, "Thank you, God, for the gift of hope. As we light the Advent wreath today, may its light remind us that when hope seems far away, you are near to us. May we nurture the light of hope in our world. Amen." You may also want to invite a group to prepare a similar presentation for putting away the Christmas greens. After the business of the Christmas season is over, it is good to give thanks for the simplicity of a "January house."

LITANY FOR LIGHTING ADVENT CANDLES

The following litany is taken from the hymn "O Come, O Come, Emmanuel." May be spoken or sung by one or more and the congregation may respond as candles are lit.

ADVENT—WEEK 1:

O come, O come, Emmanuel

And ransom captive Israel

That mourns in lowly exile here

Until the Son of God appear.

Rejoice! Rejoice! Emmanuel

Shall come to thee, O Israel.

All: Come, Lord Jesus, Come!

ADVENT—WEEK 2:

O Come, Thou Rod of Jesse, free Thine own from Satan's tyranny

From depths of Hell thy people save

And give them victory o'er the grave.

Rejoice! Rejoice! Emmanuel

Shall come to thee, O Israel.

All: Come, Lord Jesus, Come!

ADVENT—WEEK 3:

O come, Thou Day-Spring, come and cheer

Our spirits by thine advent here

Disperse the gloomy clouds of night

And death's dark shadows put to flight.

Rejoice! Rejoice! Emmanuel

Shall come to thee, O Israel.
All: Come, Lord Jesus, Come!

ADVENT—WEEK 4:

O come, Though King of David, come

And open wide our heavenly home

Make safe the way that leads on high

And close the path to misery.

Rejoice! Rejoice! Emmanuel

Shall come to thee, O Israel.
All: Come, Lord Jesus, Come!

SAFE JOURNEY TO BETHLEHEM

Leader preparation: The church practices hospitality all year long, every day. Each season of the church year presents a unique way of looking at God's hospitality and our own. We might not think of the season of Advent as a time of hospitality, but if we begin to think of hospitality as a time to both give and receive, as a time of creating safe spaces, suspending prejudices and judgments, then Advent can be seen as a perfect time to explore how we can create images of hospitality. Let's pursue one way of seeing hospitality during this season through the eyes of children.

How to use this idea in worship: Most churches will have a crèche and figures of the nativity, kings, shepherds, Mary and Joseph, and a manger for the baby Jesus. This suggestion lets them be part of worship with the help of the children.

On the First Sunday of Advent, gather everyone in the entrance or narthex of the church and unpack the empty stable. Unwrap the figures and talk about one. Explain that we're going to carry the empty stable into the worship space and set it up there through Advent. Talk about ways to make it a safe place for Mary and Joseph and the baby Jesus. Then have the children carry the stable and manger into the sanctuary. Assign some children to keep Mary and Joseph safe on this first Sunday of their journey to Bethlehem (somewhere not too close to the stable, because we will move them closer and closer each week). Keep the other characters like shepherds, kings, and Baby Jesus in the box for later Sundays. Maybe some of the animals could be in the stable this first Sunday. Be sure everyone understands that we are making a safe and welcome place for Mary, Joseph, Jesus, and everybody. Talk about what it takes to make people safe, welcome, and cared for.

Use this little litany to have the children participate:

One: Who is traveling to Bethlehem?

Children: Mary and Joseph.

One: Where are they?

Children: Right here! They're here.

One: Are you keeping them safe on their journey?

Children: Yes. We are.

One: Thank you, children.

Sing: "O Come, O Come, Emmanuel"

On the Second Sunday of Advent, conspire with the children to find a special place in the worship space for Mary and Joseph to be, somewhere a little closer to the stable, somewhere they decide will be safe, somewhere the children can look out for them. Prepare the children to be part of the following when it happens in the service:

One: Has anyone seen Mary and Joseph?

Children: We have! They're over here!

One: Are they safe on their journey to Bethlehem?

Children: Yes, we're taking care of them. We even have a blanket to keep them warm.

One: Thank you, children, for helping them on their way to Bethlehem by keeping them safe and warm.

Sing: "O Come, O Come, Emmanuel"

On the Third Sunday of Advent, conspire with the children to find a place in the worship space for Mary and Joseph a little closer to the stable, and also have them unpack the shepherds and bring them in and be ready for the following:

One: Has anyone seen Mary and Joseph?

Children: We have! They're over here!

One: Are they safe on their journey to Bethlehem?

Children: Yes, we're taking care of them.

One: Is anybody else going to Bethlehem?

Children: Shepherds!

One: Shepherds? How many? Where are they?

Children: There are _____. They're over here!

One: Are they safe?

Children: We're keeping them safe, and we brought a blanket for the sheep.

One: Thank you children for making them safe and helping them on their way.

On the Fourth Sunday of Advent, Mary, Joseph, and the shepherds are moving closer. The children are ready:

One: Only a few days to go. Are Mary and Joseph on their way, and are they safe?

Children: They're almost there, and they're safe.

One: Where are the shepherds? *(Etc.)*

One: Thank you, children for helping Mary, Joseph, and the shepherds on the way to Bethlehem where Jesus is going to be born. Will you be there when that happens on Christmas Eve?

Children: *(respond as they will)*

(Ask the children if they have any ideas about how we can make Jesus and everybody else welcome on Christmas Eve. You might say that we'll have to get the baby Jesus and the stable ready, too.)

For Christmas Eve at the chosen time in the service, have the children bring the shepherds, Mary, Joseph, and Baby Jesus and place them in the manger space. Thank the children for keeping everybody safe on their journey to this manger, and thank them for all they have done to make this a safe place for everybody.

Lead the children and everybody in a simple prayer:

"O God of Love, you sent the baby Jesus into the world to be a great joy for everyone. Thank you for the gift of this baby. Thank you for children everywhere. Keep all the children in the world safe. Help us find ways to make the world safe for everybody. Amen."

Sing: "Away in a Manger"

JOURNEY TO BETHLEHEM: A CHRISTMAS EVE CANDLE- LIGHT SERVICE OF LESSONS, CAROLS, AND COMMUNION

Leader preparation: The Festival of Lessons and Carols is a popular Christmas Eve liturgy that interweaves Bible readings with carols. Scripture is at the heart of the service. The origins of the service are British and Anglican dating back to 1880. It was made especially popular by Kings College in Cambridge beginning in 1918. For more information link to http://americanpublicmedia.publicradio.org/programs/festival/.

Supplies:

• "Journey to Bethlehem: A Candlelight Service of Lessons, Carols, and Communion" on pages 93–97

JOURNEY TO BETHLEHEM: A CANDLELIGHT SERVICE OF LESSONS, CAROLS, AND COMMUNION

PREPARING AND PRAYING AT THE MANGER

PRELUDE

WORDS OF WELCOME

SONG OF WAITING

(You may use an instrumental-only version of a carol such as "What Child Is This," "Silent Night," or "Once in Royal David's City," that traditionally begins the Festival of Lessons and Carols.)

CALL TO WORSHIP: COME TO THE MANGER, COME TO CHRIST'S LIGHT

One: This is the night. Look, the waiting is over.

Even now, a light appears.

You who wait in the shadows,

you who are cold, you with little hope,

you who are ready to sing, to dance,

to giggle with Good News—all draw near.

Look, the light shines!

All: **This is the night.**

Christ, kindle your light.

(The lighting of the Christ Candle)

One: Come to the manger!

At this place, on this night, the hopes and fears of all the years meet.

A child is born to us.

All those on earth and heaven, rejoice, be glad this holy night.

All: **Christ, kindle your light.**
This is the night.

All (singing): *"Light of the World"*

Light of the world in us re-veal, All that our eyes can never see.
Show us a world, joyful and free. Light of the world.
Light of the world bring last-ing peace. Jus-tice and mercy for the weak.
Show us the paths our lives must take. Light of the world.

PRAYERS AT THE MANGER AND PRAYER OF OUR SAVIOR
What prayers do people bring this evening? (Offer prayers for the people and allow silence to identify the prayers they bring to this night.)

PASSING THE PEACE OF CHRIST
(Invite the congregation to turn to one another, introduce themselves, and offer words such as "May God's peace be yours.")

HEARING AND SINGING AT THE MANGER

CHILDREN PREPARE THE MANGER
(Children are invited to come forward and place straw in and around the manger.)

First Lesson	*God's people long for hope.*	Isaiah 9:2, 6–7
	"Silent Night"	
Second Lesson	*The angel Gabriel speaks to Mary of Jesus.*	Luke 1:26–38
	"Lo, How a Rose E're Blooming"	
Third Lesson	*Mary visits her cousin and sings the Magnificat.*	Luke 1:39–55
	"My Soul Gives Glory to My God"	
	(Verses 1, 4 & 5)	
Fourth Lesson	*During the political power of Rome, Jesus is born.*	Luke 2:1–7
	"O Little Town of Bethlehem"	
	(Verses 1 & 3)	

| **Fifth Lesson** | *Angels and shepherds celebrate the holy birth.* | Luke 2:8–14 |
| | "Hark! The Herald Angels Sing" | |

Sixth Lesson	*Shepherds come to the manger.*	Luke 2:15–20
	"The First Noel"	
	(Verses 1–2)	

CHRISTMAS MEDITATION
(Followed with moments of silent prayer.)

OFFERING OUR GIFTS OF LOVE

OFFERING OUR GIFTS

OFFERTORY SPECIAL MUSIC

DOXOLOGY
(All sing refrain to "Angels We Have Heard on High")

Glo---ria-a, in ex-cel-sis De-o.
Glo---ria-a, in ex-cel-sis De-o.

CELEBRATING AT TABLE AND MANGER

COMMUNION PRAYER

One: God be with you.

All: **And also with you.**

One: Lift up your hearts.

All: **We lift them up to God.**

One: Let us give thanks to God.

All: **It is right to give God thanks and praise.**

One: Amazing God,
Creator of light, Giver of all life, Source of all love,
Thank you.
Scandalous God,
for giving yourself to the world
not in the powerful and the extraordinary
but in weakness and the familiar:
in a baby; in bread and wine.

Thank you,
For offering, at the journey's end, a new beginning;
for setting, in the poverty of a stable,
the richest jewel of your love;
for revealing, in a particular place,
your light for all nations…

Thank you,
for bringing us to Bethlehem, House of Bread,
where the empty are filled,
and the filled are emptied;
where the poor find riches,
and the rich recognize their poverty;
where all who kneel and hold out their hands
are unstintingly fed.

Thank you for Jesus—the child of hope, born for all.
So we join with angels singing, shepherds rejoicing, and
all of heaven and earth to proclaim this holy birth.

All: (All sing refrain to "Angels We Have Heard on High"
Glo---ria-a, in ex-cel-sis De-o.
Glo---ria-a, in ex-cel-sis De-o.

One: Holy are you, known in Jesus, Babe of Bethlehem,
Wonderful Counselor, Prince of Peace,
Teacher, Savior, Friend, Living Lord.

We remember when Jesus ate with his friends.
He took bread and after blessing it, broke it, said:
"Take, eat, this is my body given to you.
Eat this in remembrance of me."

Then he took a cup and, giving thanks,
passed it to his friends saying:
"Drink. This is the cup of the new covenant
which is poured out for you and many.
Drink this in remembrance of me."

Ever-present God, around this table
we are united in Jesus, our Emmanuel.
We are no longer strangers. We are sisters and brothers all.
And so we declare:

All: **Christ has come! Christ is here! Christ comes again and again!**

BLESSING OF BREAD AND CUP

Sharing the Bread and Cup
(While the congregation communes, the congregation may sing additional favorite Christmas carols.)

PRAYER AFTER COMMUNION *(in unison)*
Holy God,
for this journey to manger and table,
for your bread of hope, your cup of blessing,
for Christ born to us this night,
thank you. In Jesus' name, Amen.

LEAVING THE MANGER—REJOICING IN THE LIGHT

LIGHTING OF CANDLES
(While music plays, the congregation remains seated in meditation and prayer as candles are lit. For safety purposes, you may also have a few selected persons come forward and light candles. After one's candle is lit, each carefully lights a neighbor's candle—passing the light from the Christ candle. During this time, people are invited to recall the visit to the manger.)

CAROL "Joy to the World"

BENEDICTION

POSTLUDE

This service was prepared by Sidney D. Fowler for Hope United Church of Christ, Alexandria, VA.
The poem "Scandalous God" by Kate Compston is incorporated into the Communion prayer. Kate Compston's "Scandelous God" in Shine On, Star of Bethlehem, page 111–12, compiled by Geoffrey Duncan, © in this compilation Christian Aid 2001, 2002, and 2004. Used by permission.

MORE AND MORE
CHRISTMAS PRESENTS

Prepare to enter this experience: The season of Christmas extends through Epiphany Day, January 6. The following Sunday is the Baptism of Jesus, and then Sundays in Ordinary time follow until Ash Wednesday marks the beginning of Lent. During this time we can find ways to explore hospitality in worship. Christmas is a festive time of gift-giving and activity, but sometimes it feels like there is a vacuum in the days and weeks following. What if we would keep the giving and receiving of gifts going during the time following Christmas Day? Here is a simple idea for three Sundays of Christmas and after Epiphany. (You can decide how many Sundays to do this. The Sundays may vary with each year and with traditions.)

How to use this idea in worship: Begin with three Sundays following Christmas, and prepare a box for each Sunday. You can add more Sundays and boxes to extend the idea. The boxes can be any size you choose. Place the boxes in plain view of the congregation. Explain that the gift of Christmas is not just about Christmas, but that we enjoy the gift of Christmas all year long, for our whole lives. The presents are to remind us that we keep on receiving God's hospitality, and keep on giving it and sharing it with others. Have the children open the boxes, one each Sunday, and be part of the special time.

FIRST SUNDAY OF CHRISTMAS

Place in the box a rainbow made of colored silk scarves or ribbons and a card with the word HOPE written on it. Select one of the lectionary readings that brings a message of hope, or use the reading for the Second Sunday of Christmas, Jeremiah 31:7–14. Ask the children to open the box. Talk about how Jesus represents hope for the world. Talk about what hope can mean, and how we receive hope. Talk about what hopelessness is, and how we can carry boxes of hope to those who need it. Who might some of these people be? What hope can we bring? Sing a song of Christmas hope: "We Three Kings of Orient Are."

SECOND SUNDAY OF CHRISTMAS OR EPIPHANY

Place in the box an elaborate battery operated light, perhaps a lighted star. Select one of the lectionary readings that brings a message of light, or use the reading for Epiphany Day. Ask the children to open the box. Talk about how wonderful light is, and how it makes us happy. Talk about how Jesus brings light and happiness into our lives. Talk about how we can carry the light of Jesus in us and to others. Talk about people who don't seem to have much light in their lives. How might we share the light of Jesus with them? Sing a song of light: "Hark the Herald Angels Sing."

BAPTISM OF JESUS

Place in the box a large, beautiful decanter of water. Have a clear basin nearby to pour water into. Select one of the lectionary readings about water, ask the children to open the box. Ask the children to identify the water, and talk about how important, nourishing, and beautiful water is. Talk about water and baptism. Ask the children to pour the water in the basin and listen to the sound of pouring. Talk about how Jesus was called the Living Water. Whenever we give others some water, it is like doing it for Jesus. Think about those who are thirsty, and how we might help. Sing a song of water: "Wade in the Water."

Did you enjoy *Essential Advent*?

Prepare for the Lenten season with

ESSENTIAL LENT
HOLY MOMENTS AND SACRED EXPERIENCES
FOR YOUR WHOLE CONGREGATION

Paperback / $12.95

Order from

openwaterspublishing.com
800-537-3394